against a garden wall

meno lovenstein

the landon, bernard press
athens, ohio

proud and grateful

for my sons:

jon and doug

against a garden wall

shoot us simply through the heart— peasant
worker human beings— we do not die we never
have

      who else will plough the fields in spring
when earth hard with winter softens sweet
for men: these hands oak and lonely trust
a woman's throat breathing time: we build
her thatch and brick adult gratitude for
children and their voices

              early long before
the morning sun brightens gladly on the earth
stand him blinded and unshaved: he falls
with kind humility knowing you must face your
evening conscience and the slow stare of men
to come

        bullet through our singing heart we do not
die who else will plough the fields in spring
build for children and a woman warm blood in
living flesh for god's sweet unguent sun and
cool escape early clean against a garden wall

pilgrimage for a poem

from somewhere, oozing warm and wild,
a summer night, a gasping pelvic cry—
a poem!

       you love me, arms and legs
and grunty voice, forgiving me
for being less, myself in you and
all the years shuffling with naked
feet through my wordless thoughts,
forgive the poem not for you

gnarled tree roots near a stillness
in the lake and a friend so much you
are that there's a gift of sharing
when we're quiet, echo human to each
other, yet now a hushing sadness
for the poem you could never hear

but for a stringy bucktooth girl
leaning on a plow in iowa— she
will know

for the lanky boy in jeans
twitchy smiling out to people
what he wants them most to know

find them, little poem, whisper,
solemn with a twinkle, somewhere
on a loose and sweaty night, first
and new as every breath, life words
fled from warm and far ones to
strangers everywhere and near

early wisdom lonely

so then this warm-me it will die, a pity
for my body, a funeral I may not attend,
I am beyond all that, my only fear is that
the best of us may lose the sense of human
progress, pilgrimage to the high plains
of equality, hygiene of clear thinking,
folkways of cooperation, patience with the flesh

me? I want poems and a chance to add iota
to the cumulative dream: I like to think
at some last moment looking back I earned
my way, ohhh . . . spiritually

these are my thoughts for spring this year
the girls are troubled too in their way
the laughter is still in their bodies so they
cannot know and the prickly boys they dance
against the warm girls quizzically sensing
betrayal even in the nearness of their
willing, no eternal love these days but sad
happiness brief and physical as a kiss

I do not know if time has softened me
the darkling creep of night still finds a child
it takes the proud so long to beg knowing they
shall not be loved the more for it, the old can
feel no more, the young have not yet learned,

there is a moment in between the passage when
life can suddenly be felt, as though I had been
fingering its pulse since morning and here it is
beating in my hands like a frightened bird there is
a twilight zone between the confusion of love
and the low hum of care— it is a lonely shadow
cool oasis they wait there without pledge still
friendly timeless

                    you are so clever, in the
months ahead when I need mirage, would you put on
that little bonnet hat, remember! and be near me?

falling leaf

the river as the sun drops into the horizon
like a precious jewel into milady's casket
florentine

       the muslin smile of twilight
soft as a girl's shoulders when she cares

still hysteria of trees

          and beyond the
river's edge sheen and gurgle of the water
wide with slide

       alone and lost
as the twisting helpless twig rushing
sick and seaward, where will the madness
carry you and me and where the last moment,
jut of sand or twiggery to hold us filigree . . .

plea

keen murder in our happiness and melodic

suicide— all of us, you and I and

everywhere: we are ashamed of naked joy

we clothe it shy with hurried doubt—

coil of conscience still crawling in our garden

how many ways we kill the living tissue

of our flesh: smother every bird song

in the jungle of our nervous systems:

there is a poisoned dart flying this moment

at every living thing believing in its life

we too have done this you and I: if we know

let us uncover a kinder way of being human—

stem the angry burn of loneliness

invent a love for love we killed

and in the morning sleep as boy

and girl— young this side of death

no! no!

if tonight the droning locust
bird wing of visit quickly dead

these they shall not take . . .

the still flight of tall grass
blown by the wind, ballet rain
running down the road, trembling
night, girl in memory cold pierce
of starlight

            nor print nor word
nor bach rhythm twist of nerve
the kindly courage of our algebra

these you shall not touch!

                  though
tonight the droning locust, bird
wing of visit quickly dead

garden

for this first summer— I pretend
to remember others— conditioned
gratitude, o lord! and for the swabs
of cloud and bluing for your blanchissage
and the hair-worm of your horizon!

the thing called gothic . . .

                  the bone and plate

of early glass— or primitive

                  yea, muscle

and saltcellar . . .

I am aware of equinox as diagram

me, lord, I am . . .

                kepler and calculus . . .

eloi, eloi, lama sabachthani?
(which is, being interpreted)
my god, my god, why hast thou forsaken me?

cha! but this garden, my lord, my lord!

the rush of shadow over open fields

the slow chiaroscuro of the sun and wind

and our own too human conversion

to the wet: girl in her 'teens, antoine!

warm-warm: the subtlety of sweat

the chill and wool of summer-living

child!   child!   child!

                    this world of flowers,

these colors, these twists of infinite fern,

the defiance of the evergreens

the burlesque of the hermaphrodites

the crawl and worry of the wingy things

the cool conscience of the ivy

thy fingers mad upon the clavichord

the nausea of your talent, lord!

vesper

I wish god had made me
less like what we think he is
and more like what he is no doubt

I wish I knew his small talk
better

      I wish I were as simply
dirty as the next thing I see

I want to be cogwheel with living

not worth the wishing in a world
of steel-eye ready missiles, is it?

white cross

and now . . . well, now, there is a war
I must go away and waste a little blood:
oh, I'll come back— as me or someone else
living in my world . . . but either way forever
lost to you: I shall be older, yes, and
will have seen the other side of death . . .
in two years you will have found your boy
and lived his body through to loneliness

there will be an early summer afternoon
and flowers in a garden almost a woman's
body, children laughing from their toes,
the heavy rush of autos in the sun and
I shall say, "jean, why, jean, how are you!"

make a show of memory, hardly see me as you
stare, mingle love and strangeness in your
smile and I shall leave you, me, ha, me, naked
in time, man and sky and my friends, the dead

acolyte

I thought of me between a park bench and
the sky— stars, stars, an incidental moon,
devoted to the long lag logic of your way—
you, god, you!

       the cocklebur of shadow
mumming after earth with toothless gums
(I note it for a singer worming out veneer)
I am so sad, my lord!

       the plague of buzz
thumbing swift to index— thou art mad!—
and the roar of muscle moving through
a door, the squeal of wideness wending towards
the real

       to count the lips with a forefinger,
to visit humility upon the wings
of one's nose, a willingness to ache—
for thy sake!

lovers know the ground
is cruel to the world of bones, they bury
words beneath the breathing of the leaves,
learning the slowness of their clothes, a girl
laughing wise against the contraception
of her eyes trembles for the trinity

lord, lord, I do believe! I love thee so!

night

these cut screams of gnarled night, sore

mad swerve of blood, flood in throat-ears,

whimper mongrel puppies of still wet doubt:

cool asylum of hardness, kind forked love

of me, oh leg wide buttock sweetness of

cumulative years . . .

                going away— no-oh-no . . .

clang-awar-a-dib-a-loo

had there been angry thing at hand, bullet,

tight and through— 'squisite, needle neat, awoeee!

agony of acid rawly fire tongue insanely!

an angry thing at hand . . . there wasn't

this is morning, life again and my new sweet

me newly from the shower, thighs I love 'em,

white broadcloth shirt and dutch clean sky . . .

press: black ugh of sudden no matter sharply told,

torn tissue of footnote she did she hates him

and he's dead: death in millimeters calibrated,

sine and cosine fate, of wives and lives and

power dives— the laughing whore of net yields

morning voice rusting in the sun, piano memories

of the evening fore, leg and lap of idle talk,

my own dear vowels— kiss— of surplus value,

choking god almighty of a muscled hatred,

upchuck of simplicities, the bruise and orgasm

of collective will— and suddenly the delicate

miniature of being human, mouse curious her tongue

between her teeth, still not hungry human beings

waltzing glad for chinaware, salad ways and mayonnaise

and the sad hysteria of someone else's olive, ha, ha

and later, oh yes later— buzz— these my sleep eyes,

this is my love, about lenin too he danced on the snow—

he and I know . . .

elaine was there it hurt the way it didn't hurt—

o wooden cocaine afterwards of loving mnnn . . . mnnn . . .

when?

                              if death
what hysteria am I to look for
what gape of girl legs split
danseuses

              or time full bodies
flush awake

                    bright women with
eyes as tentacles

                    flytraps of
jungle fauna snapping shut at
contact

                    jesus, does a damned
book make us kin all the hot
world, nothing

                         life isn't going
to be, I'll be here till twilight
cows come home ringing brassy
bells in purple evening light

edge

later summer here . . . fog come inland excursional
I lay the logic of my own askance
sharply thereinto, circumcision of
a girl tropic cold, and done with palm leaf
africaine

      boombda, three four time,
moody as a shadow, sliver swift, and the bruise,
bite and memory, shorts and england!
jungle echo of a scream

           whippy! whippy!

wet logs whistle, this my arm is kind to amok
for my hand . . . a glass there, wise as india's
women, wants me with an oval mouth

smother pertinent outwings my nose
this distillate of fervor, a pillow
damp to dying: I little knew my hand
could slap this thing-girl in her face

tensile

weighing your hand

                                    you a lessening
thing what I felt was pang, metal
grief trembling inwards to a spine
wire molecular with sigh

                                              twirling
screamed a little girl, muscle of
a heart

                      tough the streeted world
fed me to my room

                                    late the whore
sound voices of a phone ductile for
a visit subtilized me out

                                    crone

laugh

            skin

first love

I love you, beautiful animal,
naked, white beast, and alive! your eyes
mute with ancient speech . . . your teeth,
the edging whisper of your inward breath,
the sleek malador of your loose square mouth—
you, warm, sweet, heavy languor, you . . .

your throat, and meaning so, your mind:
bird, bird, the tight, wee angles of your glance . . .
you, softly wildly throbbing in my hand!

hurt, you are hurt, you smile, a finger
utters wisely, and is gone, a shadow mad
with lurking screams in ivory, see,

a blue vein invites a knife . . .
                                    I love you,

my beautiful animal!

naked

child new visitor to this simple world

yes, you are, lovely as laughter,

    when the cool moon

and the edge sweet solace of summer grass

your open eyes darkly in the night

              your mouth

   jungle glad with smile

         the awkward humor of our

lonely bodies

     hysteria of your golden hair

and in my arms

      the meadow of your foolish sobs

suddenly the weakly human anquish

of your naked shoulders

        jesting fury of your pouting tears

weariness that rests its kindness in the bones

    a voice I never knew I had

    and laughter from the inside of one's lips

            hush

the well deep coolness of the sky

quiver

a kind of summer in the snow

sleep waiting for the dawn

aged white hair morning

in a snow flake moment

small as months go

yellow burn of spring

here is an armful of summer

warming the winds of sullen exile

your eyes cold and late

chilling the early music

of my love

soprano in a winter night

really winter now

two nights ago

it came in howling

with dust frost on the ground

and the wind blowing it

like alive dry point etching

up dark winter streets

there is a winter mood I have for you

by an open fire

warm quilted loyal you

the broken drag of sleeping voice

dark brown laughing yawn

pajama fingers on a pillow

ache of seeing

cold as window pane

child happy

the snow is soft as grandma's kiss

hear the thaw weeping from the eaves

autos sing in the street slush

fat sparrows nowise winter

pick quick the water spout

sun ha ha ha in the sky hi hi

girl she love with a luke warm cheek

and the sun ha ha in the sky hi hi

small etching

winter trees

naked crazy arms

a million greedy fingers

ballet in the violet-twilight

entrechats the winter hedge

curtsy low the canna lilies

whistling boy

a little learning

small as the quiver

of your lips

warm and alone as your eyes

love can hush you

now I know

bible story

and what they learned at jericho

        I won't forget

oh, no

           noise alone begets

a breach

            scream is quite a

        subtle speech

ever see a city wall

        crevice to a bugle call

             girl in doubt

        angle wait the music out

what they learned at jericho

        I won't forget

           oh, no

ZOO

shh! shh-shh!

we are animals

our eyes

watch you

time happens in us quietly

cat in our claws

body hide

look quick see!

tooth . . . teeth . . .

god's nose

stretch!

man is skin we're muscle

shh!

animals

fratricide

we have loved our blood in common talk
and twinned eternity in flesh akin:
I have loved you for the moment
of your heart and for the shadows of our
long descent

               yet this very morning
a woman I love saw you all once with eyes.
of love

       and all this day I died beside
you, hurting our blood
                        shame on you,
my brother, shame on your eyes

pouf

now here this every moment and suddenly too:
where are you
        and if you were I could say
it is this way with the world and not at all
that way with me
        but, no, like every
right thing, you have no sense of being
miraculous when you're needed
        wait late
hide like half-seen children I can see you

do you happen to know how light gray angry
the afternoon shadowed off, without so much
as half a word, leaving me, rushed as thrushes
screaming in a bush, this whole wide world to
care for until morning
        I tell you, time is
getting impudent and if we don't, we few who can,
I just don't know, I really don't . . .
        wince, wince
peter quince, I love you mad as august

afraid of you

the lonely anger of your body

spinal loveliness

morning dementia

moron in the noon

evening phobia musically sweet

me

hypnotic loyal

to the corners of your mouth

mnn bah

                              ha ha

    my heart

                  hum woozy

            aw

              aw

        sweet teeth

        bite 'em

            mnn bah mnn de la la mnn

pout

bite your lips

burn your eyes

thinking rattles in your head

like unpacked china dolls

ho, ho, my heart

how well you know—

twist twist!

ha, ha

sorreee!

and thinking rattles in your head

like unpacked china dolls

girl

tears in your eyes

I saw you

sitting sideways

in an arm chair cool with care

not me

ugly world? ugn-ugn

mad little inside you

six o'clock

                    spring snow

crazy world

                    night girl

oh, I don't know

                         dead light

    room gloom

                    phone ring

yellow supper fry

        mnn mnn

    I don't know

easter

          new earth

                pangy in the air

    girl in the warm breeze

                    sky

      oh, my darling world!

     pirouette

              early spring of cigarette

      sadness lolling in the sun

  I love you love you love you . . .

              hi, god!

tease, tease

like an animal

on his back

paw a teasing world

quickly jerky jungle doubt

toe faith

tough puff

like an animal on his back

paw

paw

stillborn

as if nirvana were any girl closing

a door and you the headlights of a pair

of eyes and this one room bishopy and dozing

a world for schoolmen euclidean and square

then we might lay a roman's sweated arm

against the tiles of our sweet government

or twang the tarnish of the long luke warm

for want of nubian or a greek lament

but shuffled as we are among the spores

of christ and slav, plastics, oil and steel

to curl the shine of marble corridors

to teeth the sizzle of an emery wheel

we can but ogle through windows of glass

remarking the humor of an edited mass

come and visit us in autumn

october is a lucid month

mad only at its finger tips

the trees

are grieving for their leaves

a puffy

squirrel is busy busy with his world

the logs

are whistling in the fire saying time

is such a liar

we've a bowl of flaming grog

longing for the easy man

we'll laugh about our broken

heart and summery death

chatter low, laughing

warmly at the wind

come and visit us in autumn!

science and sanity

for Korzybski

for and to the human heart

        and almost
the heart, the subtle nervous shadows
of the brain
        a thing, a name and as far
as mind can see the exquisite lurk of our
infinity

        forefinger of the estimating
eye and our body as a point, nauseous twirl
of all of it, still breath and fierce clarity,
instantaneous charity, man accumulating god!

in the bone, beneath the skin, hard world in
the skein of mind, salvation in the web,
not to know thee but in lonely honesty

mail and trees

bonsoir, marco polo, I have your letters
postmarked from the round world: manila,
burma, zanzibar, a day was it in cairo,
very hot, valencia in the rain, and paris
sweet and lewdly sane

                  in flight, a sense
of standing still— audubon, a bird, a bird!

             I have journeyed too
the slow country of another human being
cut thicket of taboo, jungle twist of
sullen gods

             laid corduroy roads through
forests cold as stone

                have heard the treble
music of the dawn crawling in the grass

streamlined anxieties of space!

what is travel—

certainly the creep of kind and not the
flight of men; man and woman waiting the thaw
of their lonely selves, for the look of sudden
nearness, right as home country: or a child's
labyrinth of wonder

these are the real spaces
longer than distance: no crush of power nor
parabola of shells can shorten by a day the
slow step of neutral time

the irony in each
empire, the lasting answer to all violence

planted heel and toe a man can travel
from morning sun to evening light and not see
all there is

here, wait here

the stream is slow and quiet, a brook
and not a river

        and people are uncertain
little pebbles: life eddies round them,
widening the circles of their fixed despair

until they know about each other

            and turn

and fall, a laughter in the water,
a grieving hurry, and echo one can
almost catch

        canaan, a new canaan,
o promised land!

          and the huddled frantic
hope, waiting this side the unopened sea

thou shall bruise his heel

me? oh-no! but for so many things I love,
near every living thing, a spider death . . .

a world too filled with noise for chamber
music— watch out!

                no slowly breathing

wait, no more

          once the flesh was young as
children's knees and once the black wet promise
of the soil . . .

          but now, pompeii rigid in the
lava mass, a new moronic stare at yesterday

and morning sick from soldier's rape

                  I know,
I know, there will be another day, curious and
deep as late love— I believe!

yet now, right now,

this very moment, we huddle in the catacombs

and wait our caesars

for over two thousand

years— it seems a day— since socrates and plato

and that boy jesus

we've known the crawl

and strut of time, the humor of our winded lust

five hundred years, denying elizabeth's smile

and louis's wig, napoleon's hat and lenin's skull

a cumulating honesty, another chance

at nakedness

and with our nakedness,

the ancient easy murder!

what shall we do

with shame, dear god, what shall we do with shame!

and this is our garden

the other day, time or spring or natural
law took me nimbly by the hand and led
me through a garden

                    here's a rose— petals?
oh, a moment's genius spent upon a soft
perfection: love in water color— forever,
ah forever . . . fragile as the evening, echo
laughter of a brief escape, tearful dew
and sadness in the morning . . . are we then
too sentimental?

                    well, prissy zinnias
buttons for our masquerade, antique jewels
for an old maid's tea

                    oh, heu-heu, ha-ha,
petunias, watery girls in voile, a droopy
handkerchief and a shy remark

chrysanthemums,
bosomy and violet-scented, a huge visit
of a great aunt, enormously warm, moustachio
and a voice so rich, one waits around
expecting gifts

and now, and now these are
our little churches, the canterbury bells,
villages and country folk and linen so clean
a prayer goes starched to heaven and sings
a triumph at the angels

but, wait, let me
stoop and touch the earth— it startles me it is
so cool

you bowed to the grass, I hope,
it's proudly green and softens to our step

cuddly

the still fire

of the evening sky

luke in the morning cool

dew leaves

and charcoal trees

grass and new born eyes

a silver moon

in a gray lagoon

curbing

cold with dawn

and thin warm a girl's arm . . .

smile in the morning

sleep

birds birds

come in

visit

do

door sweet

laughter scream and you

oh, you fill a room

new as boom

sally! and she always said . . .

tommy balding in his bourbon

your legs and my legs— my darling . . .

do not leave me go away

I shall be madeira linen

feather kissed with gossip

loving

hard as morning mirror

still as her sleeping mouth

shy as a window drape

clean as a glass of milk

rough as a kitten's tongue

warm as a twist of love

sad as the hour hand

my darling

love

o tender presence nowhere seen!
beloved touch of dear friend there
shadow bird against the green

grow destiny from what we are
laughter from the night we died
conquest in the body proud
dissolving so the need for pride

o tender presence nowhere seen
shadow bird against the green

little step

I know the grass grown wild between us—
what can we do!

             look with sweet, hard distance
smiling at the stranger, a bold and awkward
nonchalance, oh do not hear me in your nearest
world!

        or if by chance our eyes shall meet
yours are as still and dark and innocent with
fright as squirrel eyes at a forest sound:

                        a word,
a cry, a scream of silence in a cold museum,
a whirlpool of love and fever twirling sharply
into pain, oh my love!

                  ah no, ah no! a warm
and easy suicide of chance, a mocking gift
of death, while ancient lovers in the leaves
sway and urge the little step, insanely small

story

I

on a day

and in this world

upon an ordinary street

I saw a girl

so lovely god drew his breath

and envied me

II

her eyes they saw me

no, not me—

˙herself in sweet placidity

III

and walking by

and living on

I heard me whisper

I love you . . .

syncope

listen to the music scream

sweet skin in violin

      anna cool soprano girl

    bassoon in the night

thud me

    heart and knee

  boom boom tympani

and viola sad sordino eight and twenty love

      clear and wet

    eyes and ears and clarinet

        noo, alone . . .

    quick yes of saxophone

married

this winter of your lips thaws in minor hum
the ancient ivory of our kissing teeth
the wooden cross of our christian faith
is gothic there— veiled woman beneath

        I have known the seven seas
        in the salty anger of your "please!"

you were then so wise after mad moments
twice jungle savage angularly crude
you knew to divest me of immortal image
you viciously vital you criminally nude

        I have known a primal isle
        in the sultry wetness of your smile

we were so weary, careful for death,
iced in the calm of indolent stress
one and yet one etched by a breeze
into the lull of our own loneliness

        I have known a fevered sky
        in the throaty wisdom of your sigh

when words are bantered in crowded rooms
I transcend in believing myself a fool
you will never know as I touch your fingers
they make me a man that they are cool

willowy

she spoke of freud and mummeries and veils

dissecting god with her long fingernails

and the askant crinkling of her speech

the demonic niceness of a screech

the tenuity of her whys

sabered outward from her eyes

as she parried steely death

with the thinness of her breath

the mouse heart of her temple throbbing

subtilized the ancient sobbing

and the serpentry of her thighs

cooled the garden of her sighs

one could read her limpid height

as the once ecstatic might

screaming out the eerie plan

of the momentary man

but the infant in her womb

etched her likeness in the gloom

till his linear aspersions

shadowed depth into her versions

till a semi-sense of brown

puckered windward from the down

till her long motherhood of sanity

sickened softly into vanity

"now, hamlet . . ."

one could feel the midnight
ache of streets, weary
of the wheels

      you know
the monotonous conviction
that god's in his heaven—
one must pardon him
the slowing of his wit
he tried to drink

because a broken heart
has always been denied him,
he bloats the hollow
of his tuxedo shirt

a cocktail shaker lies athwart
the infinitum of his art,
the solution of him still contains
the sandy suspense of his brains

although his hair is wildly
ware of here and there,
such things as rest demand
the removing of his vest

the world or whirl or whorl
this sex or hurt, the bruise
I mean the vomit taste
raw against the teeth

      I spoke with a priest
      he said god
      was much in love
      with abelard

  varying with respect to x

      a girl with blue eyes
      and a boy
      may forever
      dally coy

and this one world we may not ever know,
lady, it hath known the eyes of many men
and how they wept their liturgies of woe
and twisted mad in many a grassy glen,
mouths long since too dry for kiss or care
loll a toothless death with heavy tongues
yet what swains shall heave a loaded swear
for love immortal and with what lungs

and, lady, one last look proves the universe

      glob of lard
      fear of knife
      the next noise

un couchant des cosmogonies

non-euclidean concretion of the yew tree

flee!

> the cankers suppurate in chrome
>
> spleen is giddy in careen
>
> ashes are the crashes
>
> if you listen

da-da de da da

> she smokes a cigar
>
> in a way you'd never
>
> think

the eternal shine of patent

leather shoes, I wonder

a sense of humor built between

a headache and sore gums

sadness feverish in the middling

behind his head a bedroom door

canters cubical, a girl's nose

disowns her sleeping mouth

> faint and noddy
>
> he loved the tightening
>
> of his body

my friend beside me knew as well her dress

was flowery voile: though walking plaster

pavements you may know the syncopation

of heel and toe a sense of rubber lies

between the hysterias of our sweet careen

we knew we could not ever feel the round

thigh and the buttock mound for these springs

of jerk and mood were flesh too wise and cruel

to brood— the truth, I said the truth, the truth

will never easily be known (they were steaks

that were her back) for all our talk or else

the bone is wizen and the wind is slack:

his eyes were warm with thinking, not at all,

he said, aristotle may even yet be right

and many bastards still among the dead,

for time and tide (a creep of lazy cloth

was sloth) and shakespeare prove a point:

I nodded, was ashamed, and understood

a sound will whistle through a town

that is to say (her chest concave with invite)

we must take care that what we say is true

my friend beside me knew as well her dress

was flowery voile: we were aware, spoke wisely,

were respectful, remembered the dying gaul,

thought twice, were happy and lived on— still

(breasts that were not were her belly) life

is cruelest to be kind: when next we spoke

the theme had turned (we scarcely breathed to learn

her kneecap whispered toughly through the silk)

arms wide

the slow fingers of a cloud

grew upon the moon

her body, the night, is chill

is still

the air— her hair

my breath— her mouth

the sky my love!

ah, slow the fingers

soft the fingers

grew upon the moon

funeral

a woman with a face of naked flesh
she was so tired her body slept inside
her clothes her bones were lewd in private
ache

      men in cloth and darkened women spoke
of life et cetera

                a small room with standing
people moves us to uneasiness a cough is
sacrilege

      dear life, sweet thing, ah me!

and wherefore violence, you my late love
whom I hurt or you poet and your several
lines— what of our moments or must we never
know the mild denying coolness of the dead

          woman, broken thing,
these my eyes speak to you as I grasp your
hands

      the loosely hanging muscles of
your arms are real the touch of wooden doors
is good to know

      and oh I love the crazy
sweetness of this summer day

honeymoon

as though life were a wind-blown spray
and time as billowy as faraway trees
in june

            her eyes half-closed and still
and laughter from the gladness in her hair
and teeth and finger tips

                his body heavy
in love, unmasculine with tender joy: strong
too strong

          o wild nakedness and sudden
stranger

      lipping curve of knowing— day words
strange as night

          and sadness waiting in the room
like roses one day old . . .

             do not leave me, o my love!

cock-a-doodle-doo

wake, my sweet, the morning sun
touseled sheets are swearing
cool the shadows of the night
whisper low and daring

my love, my love, your sleepy hair
limbs akimbo every way
shameless, lazy, weary
saddened in our play

ah, my drowsy little darling
passion all for yawning
pouting puffs of soft rebuffs
to the silver dawning

flicker

oh, I know, a woman, a nipple, a night,
and love such as men never have known—
absurd little miracle only for me

nooo . . . I will live in the gloom of music
and mind, a ghost of myself by a cooling
fire, the sick tick of an ancient clock,
and a hound with twice closed eyes

with pistol points at the thing, my brain

and three years old, a soldier boy saying,
I will!

    and a little girl with womanly hair,
a winter ash tree in a story book storm

and a man with a stroke who stared at me

spring loneliness

the grass I think is crazy this year

it's soft and whispers in the wind

the pebbles I think are sad this year

and the leaves don't care

a robin tugged at a sullen worm

the ivy's cooler this year I think

and the trees are wooden and the leaves don't care

menu

in a yellow coffee shop

while the music listened

you laughed touching the corners

of your mouth with napkin point

and finger tips

                    the wild girl

in your eyes and the soft kiss

of your shoulders

                         oh how we held

the world tantrum in our arms

deaf-mute

hide the silence with your noise, go, go,

do not listen, do not hear the whisper

of an autumn leaf blown lonely by the wind,

the cool cry of early morning, dark music

in experienced eyes, girl muscle when she

laughs, unheard the thump of steady blood,

mortal rasp of throat and lung, crackling

murmur of the atoms, envy and her

meditative teeth, nations and the

sharpening steel, oh, listen to the

silence, hush and listen to the silence

battle hymn

gust of earth

          scream soldier

mother mother!

          kill the living thing

before you

        smile him sweetly to his grave

leave the blade breathing in his throat

we love the open mouth of flesh

the insane throb of naked heart

we bleed the pulse of river blood

                  pity us, lord

pity the media of your brutal art

a way

there is a way, commit your suicide
each moment by not living it,
we never do exhaust ourselves,
love with a love we have for
others, cruel sweet and paw heavy

to live as though the flood of
things to come were dammed against
a body's life

                    peaked for whispers
wind blown from valleys far beyond

you love us, sad as the blood stream
keen as the next orgasm, you will
survive this world, commend us gently
to utter strangers, they will come,
tell them we were not ready for
our living, pathetically heroic,
we abused our lives, now shy in
unmarked graves we wait out time

anesthesia

well, it's this way, there can be too much,
shall I explain, why, then too much of
people dying and fire and hurt and noise
and tear and pretty girls still puppy blind
and doing, too much of that, and going
and coming, hammering and torture twisting
in a screwdriver and, oh yes, sunlight
and the rain, too much of what there is
because we are as anxious to grow poor
as we are to grow rich

                    am I paris
taken, an open city and a closed hope

gentlemen, this is no time for division
of the spirit, now and perhaps for the last
time we are fighting for our lives, our
liberty and our sacramental honor . . .

the virus having long lain waiting

for such a rise to power sees in a

tyrant and those who would deny him

just the chance to multiply his kind

and spread throughout the world with

such understatement . . .

                           the curfew lately laid

upon us finds us deep abed before it rings,

there is no end to the subtlety of

compliance, milady legs apart observes

indignity hath its pleasures, so and so,

have you heard anything to the contrary

bicentennial — u.s.a.

now days whirling by like paint-gay

wooden horses on a merry-go-round

while the calliope whines a national

anthem and the circus tent sick noises

of our centuries fever in the neon

sky red with shame

                                               three million square

miles america forever adolescent,

muscle sure of food and space, gangling

free as though liberty were nature's

breath ho-ing westward without end

brute injustice and glow forgetfulness

absolved from guilt by flippant charity,

abrasive kind and harshly gentle, salves

of things upon the bruise of privacy

sunday morning god twenty minutes and

an organ, a christmas need for poverty,

a tolerance for babbling faiths

and tax-free hopes

                              innocent

illiteracy ringing school bells

oh but the gift of its disorder,

the cryptic sanity, fumbling wisdom

and the awkward honor, irreverent heir

to all the treasury of the western

mind, and still a chancy beachhead

stone

we have our winter now, not the winters
of new york, piercing and ragged cold,
torn by skyscrapers into shreds of despair

nor southern winters, more a man's old age,
sunlight playful on the evergreens, teasing
warm for painful bones with chilly greeting
from the benches and the public fountain

new england too, only colder summer,
a village snow a man can come to love,
sane calm mildly angry motherhood
softly hard with wordless courage

but ours in minnesota they are brute
these solid massive winters, a bitter
woman of forty, there is no way to
plead with her, kindness only defines her
loneliness and love it cannot prosper
because the cold comes through the walls
and windows and sits between the legs

hmm-hmm

in this old world

                            wild new

craaazy puppy!

jingle-jungle in our eyes

fatty slappy in our thighs

willow! willow!

time and pillow

trees leaves

paranoia breeze

puppy wuppy mitten kittens

wuppy puppy kitten mittens

hug-a-body

hug oh tight

bone alone

world around us: boo

hurty sweety sweaty ooze

flesh is angry love a bruise

deadly darling

doubly dear

morning lips

and summer hair

knees are simply everywhere

go away

snow snow go away snow

        drizzle drizzle weary gray

    sad furniture

        generations old

no one whose heart

        is deep alone

        sick new with night

    I laugh you say damp fire I know

      so go away snow

death wish

here then

upon a cliff

edgy fragile and alive

oh nipple cloud

soft mother sky

and nowhere heard

a lullaby

remembering

from beneath the earth of me
a startled here am I again
so come, my hand, come sway along
skip wildly where a time there was:
cold rocks on naked feet in curling
brooks in spring, dog a-drooling love
in catchy breath, sweet loneliness
with oneself and poems tenderly alive,
bold boy hand on a shy white breast
and a wing-tipped smile of her early love,
a moon and a star and a whistling night
september sun and a brother's death
then suddenly always you, my love,
dying adagio for a fleshy moment—
but oh, oh my loving god my sons!
now the shadows creeping cool
as quietly breathing ivy over
dark window panes gently lays
a wisp of silence on my eyes

tiff

words— they

cannot unsay

what words have said—

that life is dead

but caring most

about a ghost

can make a wife

of daily life

and bodies warm

can do no harm

when sudden heart

and legs, an art

beg for pardon

in a garden

and laughter deep

gentles words asleep

solstice

if april is the cruelest month

then not for baby finger buds

nor meadows greening for the touch

nor warming flesh alive for skin

sweet rain upon an open face

and soft wild big dipper night

but hurting numb the winter chill

courage hardened in the bone

a mummy of memories aping

summer near a fire, a sudden fall

of ashen logs, a frost upon new hope,

leaving us yes oh one and all

late lovers of our only lives

heart attack

easy queasy

                live on teasy

      sallow young

             echo lung

hollow tender

        breathing slender

      beggar wise

           asking eyes

the seasons: male eyes

spring? a girl, her hair, warm night
laughter and feverish smooth her skin,
all and none of her, a-child-a-woman,
a bite and kiss, suddenly wild chatter
then a pool of silence and an empty stare

summer, the quick thin joy rounded into
woman, the foliage of her secret
loveliness, small tired with birds, deep
heat in her body, time afire, horizon
in her hair and echo in her eyes

lonely autumn, golden fingers hard and
kind, humor of the rouge and gold,
brown the down of wise sad skin, remember?
yes, of course, I do, we were there! dark
trees, whispering bushes and the eglantine

a woman's winter, children borne as
earth and flesh, pain and love umbilical
and a hollow heart, mother to the
father and a sisterhood with god, in
weariness, mutely angry and forgiving,
discovering too late who she really was

when needed

listening softly

　　　　　quietly with care

wispy within me

　　　　　closely out there

tenderly awkward

　　　　　sighing no words

creature loving—

　　　　　dog human and birds

anguish

only when with all my heart

I cannot love enough the warm

wide gust of western mind

woman-man of jesus-calculus

workers' hands animal with matter

ghetto eyes where huddled time

moans the dirge of each man's pain

only when I lack the art

to crumble museums into agony

and canvas, flog the high priests

of the frontal lobes, flout

rule sick designs of logic

into nauseous honesty,

waken ancient cultures

stink-smug in new world hells

only when with all my heart

only when I lack the art

birth cry

we are the slumbering seeds hidden
in the winter earth, the torrents
still frozen in the glacial wait,
the desert sweetened on the young—
the world's to come alive again

we are the hurt and gladness,
people, people everywhere:
the lonely dead, the swarm unborn,
music still unheard, and throbbing
old love in fresh one-time bodies,
happy baby skin sucking mama skin,
garden fingers loving soft the earth,
erectile tissue answering time

the human rush of spring floods,
dark cool of forests, birth scream
of open sky, monstrous thighs of
mountains and silk warm valleys,
forgiven pain and love— for breath

three

dangling by a mother's hand
dragged umbilically along

lookie lookie button eyes

a smile from inner me
to all of you

        a twig of
wonder then a bud of love

twist-a-twist to keep a joy

        bye bye little boy
        bye bye happy man

echo

tuning forks for the listening dead
hammered into hum by pulses echoing
through ruins

      muted cries that seemed
to die and thoughts still trembling
in mausoleum skulls

        the nervous edge
of stillborn love

       sound and color
faraway beckoning with ghostly tease

while in the world as womb the fetal
prayer listens to the muffled throb

now

now is not the shadow of a tree
before the sun has peaked nor after

sad in sullen aging eyes
lips bitten softly into thought

not tensely finger tips from yet ago
a woman's lolling hair oh where

now is feverish warm orgasm love
the sun at noon blinding gratitude

nightmare loving

oh, ha, ha, what are you doing
on the window ledge teasing
a kitty kat and that hat it must
belong to someone else but I
remember loving you

                      you, not you,
did you really have to die before
we finished talking

                     oh, no!
watch out, what happened to that
falling thing

                water bubbles
on your breast, guilty eye,
estranging odor in your hair I care

I was to wait I know but the sun
chuckled on the chandelier

so many many as though you never were

chorus girl

mask smile and eyes of glass
leggy breastie pink and white

teeth rimmed in brazen red,
hair to beg for softened love

muscle body bold and hiding,
long thighs flowing into toes

girl and woman inside men
laughter in between the sexes

oh third from left in puppet row
we two alone in our own night

marigolds in autumn

alien seed from mexico
flower citizen long ago

peasant color in a garden
for the sun a petal pardon

for a visit people border
scentless in the floral order

in the autumn summer bright
stiffening with winter fright

weedy wooden in the snow
manana from old mexico

far

you touching close
but do not hear

oh, this good thing
it came to me

oh, one more death
I want to share

a warm wind, please,
mouth corners twitch!

halloo halloo

you need someone
so you can hear

illness

sunshine waiting shyly on the window panes
and flowers smiling gently without words,
books too heavy to be opened and the clock
whispering time like a child's secret

fever making into two the body's
loneliness for love, pain discovered
with surprise in the dark catacombs
of being alive, a weariness bleeding
slow and softly into thin devoted sighs

apologetic visitors vertical
to death, forgiven enemies, lightly
offering tomorrow pinched between
thumb and forefinger, squeezed eyes
awkward care and numb tedium prayer

thing

have you ever seen a "thing"

lonesome for your eyes

patient where it is

stillness almost wise

an ash tray or a person

waiting to be seen

shyly in the world

grassy in the green

old man

softly thin and slow, dimly still alive
mumbling at the shadows in his head
and gray around

                musing at the warm sun,
grandchild on his skin

                   a baby smile for
squirrels

           for brashly young a teen age
girl a love suffused and gentle for the
heart and not the fork of her

                   and for a
stumbling person in the wind, an auto
screeching error, a broken tree limb
or an orphan leaf, a helpless comprehending
gaze, the last word unuttered on the cross

beautiful woman

droopy theatre wings, applause
smack white flesh with open palms

uglify the music, whore in more

hugging smiles over blinding
lights, arms-wide love for no one

oh, but I will be a creaking
door in your haunted house

etude for four hands

prostrate I am one lonely corpse
waiting for jesus in a rented room—
the tongue in prayer, o most cathedral!

your smile is ancient, once an angry boy
in asia minor swam too far against the sea

hands are not so subtle as a floor
a persian rug is ghetto, hush, my love!

my majesty upon a cushion couch,
chromium bejewelled with points
of sunlight, wood silk in the sheen,
gossamer of idiom, impudence
of window glass, steel miming at the ice,
a trying in the braid, the noon day hour
lolls like girls in summer dresses

with this cigarette I singe the venus
mound of an ash tray dancing girl— no
plaiting forward of our rhythms may deny
the lewd saga of a woman whispering
laughter from the caverns of her eyes

ingratitude

and this is a let-go letter, lonely music
muffled in the drapes, wanting to be heard

sadly a cigarette vaguely in my hand,
for a thinking mouth

                    I'm scared need hang on
love you

            where now the frenzy warm sweet naked
love cuddling silence too near an open fire
while the flames made funny clowns, the shifting
logs a whimsy fright

                    now you are everywhere,
a smothering competence, cushions of late summer
care, a softer bosom and a hardened laugh
and queenly a ridicule of all complaint

etching

curling cry of over table love

silver in a satin world

sullen anger amber skin

warm cream of waiting arms

schizophrenic thighs

naked bodies native cruel

hushing burn of midnight fire

shoulders rounded into yoke

voices word and word cooling

in a room, talking low to quiet

a little girl, mirror humor

boomba boomba laughing death

boomba boomba sadly boomba

brother's suicide

the wind blown hair of chaos
hysteric smile and bullet
time bleeding in a pool
still glass eyes half open
contemplative of the living

silence without wanting
escape from need and love
a gift of icy guilt
numb confusion into grief
burying an unspent life
in an earth of helpless care

quarrel

cold as winter water

gray eyes in a stare

mouth a little smaller

arms forbidding breasts

thoughts in angry furrows

words no one can say

glances at a still clock

moonlight on a grave

do not make a stranger

of our fumbling selves

the crocuses we planted

will blossom early spring

civil war

a dead man with a mouth half open
hatred untouchable in a corpse,
inviolate of all indignity,
beyond forever the hope of echo,
a face no more, spilling mockery
of blood, a silence of humanity

smiling down a live man with a lust
still to murder death points a trigger
angry gun at his enemies not yet
dead, clatter cry of torn space,
defeated steel into pulpy flesh

the dead man and the live one, if the
dead they will not die, if the dying
is the living, if the living is
the dying, if the cradle is the tomb,
if the grave rocks the cradle, if the
loving is the hating and the hating
is the loving, if the dead man and
the live one, if the living and the
dead, comes the end of it at last

spring storm

crawl of tree roots snugging earth
leafy limbs wildly ballet in the wind
scowling skies mumbling thunder
whimsy lightning jaggedly exciting

scurry of the little things, children
edging towards a mother, timid grass
thatched against a wooden fence
shyly first drops quickly rain

then as though it did not happen
dried tears for a moment's anger
naked air, cleanly green, and
impish laughter oh somewhere

and in the west

eyes as wide as all the sky

loving arms lonely for the world

quiet glow of blue and gold

wild fire in a shroud of clouds

bowing low the one day sun

orphaned people waiting time

stand of stillness fore the dark

cool air whispering to the night

and the night hiding in our rooms

ghost people

tired feet strangers at a bus stop,
leaning on themselves, alive a minute
in a weary smile

         glass partitioned
bodies, eyes upon a slab of desk,
bartering life for words and numbers

parents after growing up is done

sons and daughters alien in time
as men and women

         brothers sisters
too long in the world together

          friends
who were not before they were and will
not be when the road turns a little

lovers in the morning light

         anyone
a corpse searching for a happier moment

human faces

mirrors for a mirror world

asking for a love or hate

pond and stream of animal eyes

teeth, teeth lastly civilized

mouths chewing warm meat words

noses for the comedy of air

ears for whisper and alarm

begging cheeks hiding bone

chins confessing everything

tears and terror infant smiles

flash surprise of hiding selves

open for a love or hate

mirror in a mirror world

amber bracelets

forty in her loveliness
brown and spiny thin and
yellow gold, her hands
I swear subtilize the
evening air and her fingers
cool and wise lattice
through her waiting eyes

her voice whispering
contralto and she smiles
as though the morning was
too early in the night
and her laughter oh
promising no memories

waitress

water with a pregnant smile
food breasty warm and near
mama mouth fumbling frantic
for the nipple of a menu

sleepy lover tummy full
teasing after dinner love
looking eyes do not see
dreamy distant wedding bells

demolished

sweaty skill in stone and wood
bleeding time into design
nature used against herself
windows walls and winking doors

rough and hard the human touch
etching shoes and finger nails
plaster aging into flesh
fashion weary curlicues

steel ball on a manic crane
pitiless in downward thunder
dignity crumbled in the rubble
another day wounded into silence

end of a novel

when first you came into my eyes,
shadow lives in prose and talk,
I gazed with champagne humor
pretending you might be alive

but you were stealing into me
with your shy and naked thoughts
and we were happening alone
in a purr of love and care

now you are gnarled driftwood
jagged smooth from angry seas
stilled agony crying in the wood
and I have come alive to grieve

goodbye

wordless at the shore's edge
a life of love frenzy silent
in a stare of far horizon

bodies agonizing into two
pain and dark room loneliness
lovers now a brother sister

one ache of moment more
startled at a need to move
a hurry of eternity

coldly free from dying
echo laughter slowly bleeding
and a sea shell for the ear

skin

between the blood and mystery of me
and all those wavy particles pounding
on my own existence, thankee for my
two faced skin, motherly protective
of the inner child, embracing arms
against the world's unclear intent

and for the skin on bones wherever

baby skin warm innocence of birth,
time before the counting starts

teen age skin feverishly erectile
surly and alone in nature's love

woman's skin asking someone to be
kind, friendly still if they are not

a man's skin military in a silent
war, wondering why his muted rape
does not cradle his sweet fears away

aged skin old lace weary wisdom
smiling at a memory of muscle

brown yellow black and white pigment
tease, color taunt, palette of the sun
and genes, laughing at divided man

plain girl

oh she's there and warm and wanting

wifey eyes not full of men

lips and teeth for honest smiling

breast and legs for what they are

a darker music in her voice

when she cares a moment pretty

early woman of the earth

work hands kneading time and love

faces

on any street I gaze

happy that you are alive

greeting eyes with eyes

strangers sharing faces

a smile from within

tears about to cry

worrying a wrinkle

bitten lonely mouths

magic of a new face

for a sudden friend

hard unseeing seeing

sheathing privacy

oh I love all faces

naked in the world

resembling someone

I know that I have known

cold night

stone still the open hearth
small stage of ballet flames
shadows pirouette a smile

quiet talk of burning wood
warmly moody memory
and a wanting to be kind

serious one

I love her love her, teeth and titty,
will always love her legs and twitty—
why are you smiling buddha buddha?

I am I am my brow is frowning
in dignity I'm slowing drowning—
why are you smiling buddha buddha?

I died one day for something live
believing two and two are five—
oh why your smiling buddha buddha?

granny glasses

lips belonging to a mouth
straight hair working woman
farm eyes feed a family
and her smile a crease of pain
wearily a frown of humor
long skirt for her churchy legs
mother smell from her body
a kiss to warm a chilly room
and her bearded boy and man
high arch gaze gently honest
people as they might have been
if only nothing happened

nursing home

lullabies for an open grave

trembling hands in a fuzzy world

early memories smilingly alive

mushy chatter almost echoes

childish anger in a corner

laughter trailing off to sigh

clinging to the moments when,

honoring life by wanting it,

live epitaphs to dignity

hiss

open wide and sleepy sure
cuddled quiet with love and trust
proudly tall because I cared
smiling warm to think of you

then angry keen your venom words
coiled darting snake quick sting,
my terror disbelief and panic
search for something dear— and gone

a winter beach of sad exile
slow funeral for a sighing wound
why-not laughter from a clown
and older love cagey caring

black cat on white satin

oh, pooh upon your mystery
paws folded inward to your pride
green eyes do not bewitch me
arrogance can be denied

but then why so queenly fed
did a kitten's puffy play
put it in your mystic head,
without a whine, to go away

faithless

all those years I trusted you, a child
in the warm silence of your body,
even when alone bewildered on a
cool unmarried pillow, when tender glad
to share a thought or sorrowing for
a distance, memories of the middling,
sweet shadows of a sigh, the grateful
throaty moan and the soiled and lonely sadness
of our naked sleepy skin

                        I remember,
bedded in a father's proud appraisal
of his sons, tall as men, once the rounded
tummy of a leggy girl, your whimsy breasts
now mother woman milky, my smile loving
all of you, your busy frown and stronger hands

oh, the morning hair and evening gowns
the crinkly smiles for stranger friends
harsh laughter for a sobbing world— you
drew away from all that's near, a molten

anger always teasing in your eyes,
the knuckles of your fingers tapping
out the frantic rhythms

                   then from around
the curvy sound of rumor, a cry of shattered
certainty, you were sleeping against another—
a loathsome crawl of eels, whispering
music for an easy suicide, a hollow
bleeding in a shroud of tears, grimaces
knifey kind and cold flesh everywhere
whoring solace

            and what of you and rented
love, tumbling in confusion and a flaunt
of murky freedom, tedious in wrinkled sheets,
waiting old for moments young, a memory
of what there was loosening a wordless
mouth

         forgiven as the dead forgive
closed eyes stillness and a wooden grief

thoughts upon a bed

oh mother lover rumpled sheets
now lay me down my weary bones
padded don't you worry none
just you rock a bye to sleep

oh mother bed I love you so
yawning for to hear a story
shadow stranger in the night
fumbling for a streak of boy

spread eagle woman waiting
in the glisten of her eyes
and a man almost a minute
pillow puffy lover bed

wake

death, sweet chit, g and e string,

calmly grotesque, the playful

suicide of moving things

helpless skirl of motored steel,

the complicated candor

of a friend, the crawl, the creep,

the filigree, prosy chain

of you and me, the sky lie

of circumstance, millions

of frantic fingers, grasping

the earth's edge

                    sneak thief, before

you know, time slips by with half

your life hid underneath his arm

taste it burning in your throat

find her feverish in the night

wallow weepy for the wounded

step lightly when there's god around

hug yourself a little tighter

stare new wonder at the stars

a day in april

spring, shy warm girl in calico,
we walked your puppy earth, dusty
sweet and slow tired, we heard
the sigh of open land, hurry
water murmuring to pebbles
and jumping squirrels twiggy
in the air, soft the silence
of butterflies caressing
noon-day flowers

                we lay upon
the ground and let the sun make
love to us, our eyes were closed
for privacy, there was a hush
of music in our arms and legs,
and thinly near a veil of sadness,
the cool edge of a setting sun

upon a cross

human beings I love you so
the forest shadows of your thoughts
the pulpy pity of your flesh,
woman oh yes woman, the soft
and subtle solace for all dying,
the hunter blessing murder with
his hunger, escape between
divided waters, new tender god
in dark catacombs, braided prayer
strutting gold in vaticans,
the inward journey of the mind
uncovering order from a demon
world, children laughing screams
of doing, shy 'teen breasts in a
bathroom mirror, cocoon boy emerging
into man, candy sweet the bridal
kiss, the pelvic cradle mother
the weathered care of fathers
lonely sore the hum of fever,
the silence of time breathing
and the still alive in human
death, I love you oh I love you

mozart

the hum and lilt of
happiness twirling
in the shadows of
smiling candlelight

pointed toe and wink
laughter near to tears
childhood late and soon
the sky if it could sing

big city

shredded people shadows,
silent strangers on hard
streets, doggy lovers lonely
linked to furry busy warmth,
the pulsing cry of ambulances
screaming out the agony
of open flesh somewhere
bleeding on the concrete

the skyline of flaunted
wealth, the window tease
of fantasy and greed, faces
cold and anxious, flat humans
vertical to love, and the
million city peasants
grubby at the smelly tasks

paint dirty artist hands
made precious in stone museums,
music from the trembling ear
dulled in elegance and echo,
the ready whore and saint
of talents now and long ago

trap and web of too much

breath, a feverish sludge of

all humanity, one thud

colossal of ejaculating

hope, a massive organ of

despair and anesthesia

saved only by a baby's eyes

smiling a wonder and the

budding leaves of trees

uncomfortable in public parks

pornography

warm eyes looking inward
on cold naked pity skin
soft and wounded bodies
manikins of empty love

tweaky lonely fever
begging to be human
muffled fleshy whimper
in a swamp of need

monkey grimace swinging
touchy mimic in a cage
blood it races wildly
panting nature's whimsy

judge not

a tombstone face with eagle eyes,
flesh bone skeleton in begging clothes,
trapped rigid wild in fear and anger,
wounded fierce, he stands and stares

hurt and hounded into sullen pride,
shrouded silent in a sightless world,
he cannot weep to murder warmth
killing for a chance to die

grieving shadows, hiding from the sun,
whisper hoarsely in a catacomb
of care, black veils sighing,
helpless wisdom in a common grave

wisp

a billion years— and me, come now,
wild fling of genes chuckling pity
for my body helplessly alive,
a tweaky jump of ions into pain,
love a panic squeeze of fantasy
clinging darkly for a miracle
to another fragile no one

the deaf mute silence of the stars
the snakey slither of cold time
lizard memories in primeval grass
mothering hunger from the sea

how warm how soft your fever skin
the hush and whisper sound of night
a wink of living and a sigh

jet around the world

purring wait, committed rush to leave the earth,

then oh and ah, bird winging into air,

inhuman power absurdly quiet,

motors with round open mouths sucking space,

a smile at large things growing small, the mother

bed of bosom clouds, god's whimsy rivers

and his mountain toys, roads brothering

the loneliness, cargo people hostages

to embodied genius, the royal

luxuries rootless to the peasant world,

and speed the sly illusion of being near

stranger faces on familiar bodies, walking

blind through visiting eyes, girl quizzing

on brute concrete, grey people humbly waiting

red or green, embarassed flowers remembering

the soil and the sun vainly peering into

window museums

oriental faces slowly
turning into separate human beings,
black and white anxiety inner looking, almost
never never a happy sharing face,
babel tongues estranging love, while the words
sigh and cry and laugh the pity wonder
oneness of all flesh

weary of the empty sky,
homesick for the earth, fearing its avenging
patience, the small, like growing children, adults
all at once, belted faith tombstone upright,
new love for the ancient ground, wheels birth pang
clutching, power raring slow to calm the blood,
home a distant land, the world a neighbor's house

taj mahal

when I traveled far to embrace
your loveliness, the monsoon skies
were grey and gloomed upon your creamy
marble, a weep of rain remembered
all your love and grieved for you

four minarets sigh a silent prayer
to the corners of your earth, one
large bosom turret nippled love
for allah and smaller human ones
for memories

         oh, taj mahal,
the loving lift of open arches,
a woman's love, a body warm and strong,
so deep into the thrust of life
death is but a long remembering

india beggar girl

with fingers to your lips mumbling

hunger for yourself and the baby-thing

loosely in your arms, if there you are

if here I am, if misery everywhere

around can still be shared,

I suffer for my token gift

of life given in a helpless

exchange of eyes, then as you

leave me with the pity of my giving,

you walk away, the agony in your face

suddenly no more and a cunning victory

in your glance, absolving all my guilt

into a brutal glare of circumstance

cremation

once I was not in this world and soon
I'll go again into the nothing
of the flesh

          I learned to hide my falling
in a walk and at a time I slept
a dream upon another's warmth,
echo words I heard from hollowed lives
and reached out my arms to agony

now there's a silence to be listened for,
a shadow veil billowy in a cavern wind,
and I will be again unborn,
waiting not as me for life anew

tourist guide

japan girl

we are little children, yes—
no, we will not lose the bus,
oh how large that buddha is!
king mikabushi make a war?

quick white smile black star eyes
tinkle toy breath tiny nose
kimono small step western dress,
I love you, the day long tour

india

shadow people creating space through a subtle
absence of themselves, a swarm of millions
in a hush of being, the stoney ghosts of
ancient art, simplicity elaborate and
benumbing, mock tombs against all living,
golden saris sway with sensuous silence,
whispering veils subtilize the vague
uncertain momentary breathing, angled
bodies in a rooted dance of hands, symbols
of a story long ago or never, the
tamburas softly whine the muted heart,
while precise colonial english presides
with courtly manners over hindi rhythms

in the cities fanatic autos, snorting
nasal anger, weave through the slow unminding
milling and from buildings more ancient
than they are a weary smell of endless
life seeps out the air for thin bodies
squatting time away, white long face cows,
hermits of a wise and calm indifference,
deny the highways into meadows, and the
countryside almost a still-life of survival

which child shall lead them

a child always commands us, not the love
skin staring eyes and dangling legs,
but the face of childhood upon whatever
priests of certainty there are— the sweet
distance of the clergy becalmed with truth,
the plastic dedication of the military
boys, the guileless integrity of the
laboratory man

                    oh, it was bold,
all right, and tantalizing— the irrational
creep of logic vining loose the structures
of old faiths, cartesian coordinates
to corner the universe, the calculus's
inching hold on change, the full world
reduced at last to variables, that quiet
smile of pointed knowing, a grasp on god,
a new proud dignity for the mind,
power as a form of innocence,
science an ego and again the child

acrobatic gadgetry to lessen pain,
postponed for a holocaust, a fantasy
of people benumbed into numbers,
technology a cold mission of salvation,
facts pyramided high to answer death,

common sense proving common sense a proof,

understanding in a hall of mirrors,

while the mocking probabilities etch away

the confidence and more knowing shatters

the glass encasement of certainty

ah, the peaks of genius as a measurement

of man, da vinci's wonderment, david's

young courage ready for a slingshot,

hamlet and the cursed spite, the golden

shadow of rembrandt's honesty, the freshet

song of mozart, the stubborn inner

probe of einstein

for antibiotics

we whimper gratitude, for a moon fling

a bewildered pride, for miracles

a sighing fear, for a painless life

a compensating bedlam of anxiety

oh, lamb, oh, lord, oh, little one,

a child possessing us because we care,

is there wisdom in your innocence?

tomorrow but today's own toy? we ask,

wrinkling an adult brow with trusting love

ruins and museums

we are dead now, yes, we know, but
we were once alive— feel our flesh
hardened in the stones, we piled them
high for gods we loved and feared,
not for your weary tourist's gaze
bemused with time and losing precious
days in memories not really yours

rubens painted me, discovering in my
body rosy flesh and rounded folds of
warmth, it was delicious to feel his
eyes exciting me with nakedness,
so there you are observing line and
color, with awed importance just for
looking, but when the painted thing
was done, we snuggled warm in cushion
art and chuckled at you upright
below high ceilings in a cold museum

young

young is whispering nothing into
a feverish mouth, tingling tense
in warm wet skin, an alchemy
to make an old world new, o faugh!
that's not young— to shiver
not alive as nature's manikin

sunk into us all a sense of
flippancy, a casual roulette
of hopes and enterprise, a sleight
of hand with destiny, teasing
finality with a bleary eye
upon the button of damnation,
equal young and old at the
animal edge of survival,
while the nuclear bombs shake an
intoxicated finger at the universe

young, it is to be poetically
akin to time, listening for
history still unuttered,
eavesdropping on the not yet,
growing older younger to hear

the past and time's own echo, lifted
by the good cheer of the mind awake,
dizzy glad for the sad foolish
wonder of the immensity of man,
come grow younger still, younger than
the moment first, back, deep and back
into the inexhaustible thrust

tomorrow is not today grown
chill at evening— it is morning
at the shadowy end of night,
opening horizon on the shrill
amazement of another day

chirp

oh, I have seen those eyes before
and that smile, of course, but where,
the curve of some girl cuddling breasts
for a night wind's shadow boy

a gray bone man wobbling slow
and a baby finger holding,
the bathroom legs of fat women
and a bird darting sure to perch

wearily just once more again,
the world a museum for a visit,
until the tidbits of eternity
beg to be sweet loving new

pizzicato

sparkle in a blue eye

titter tonguing tease

nipple in a sweater

picky pointed chatter

ballet touchy toe

a pinky on a treble

sunbeam on the water

peaky hummingbird

snakey biting two dot

witty twitty jest

tingle in the tangle-

after loving kiss

poems

the velvet petal of a rose

sunlight dancing with the dust

still squirrel on a trunk of tree

eyes upon you without words

the surly mouth of pretty girl

old brick weather tired and aging

metal noise from a hurting thing

poems in their tender world alone

wings

a rush of migrant birds
chattering in a tree
a flutter whim of nervous
fright and they are gone

not all of them— a scatter
of the slow and busy ones
startled to be all alone
flap hurry to belong again

I am the lonely leaves and
limbs remembering the wild
excitement of a frenzy
visit and grieving for birds

snow

soft o silent falling snow
tingle on glad icy skin
bosoming the winter earth
white and wide for open eyes

little gentle flakes of time
mounding free from wheel and foot
a cold and smiling tomb of air
frostly mocking early death

window

daytime night on snow white hills
cold light moon in dark black sky
crystal icicles spear the air
footprint memories someone gone

window loneliness without tears
open book waiting to be read
piano sad bass, treble love,
a soft forgiving everything

the whole world

grabby lust for all of it
head heart and loinal ready
space arms embracing me-me
smiling faces to be used

faraway just for teasing
bee happy in a flower
temple stones of ancient hope
brochure loneliness on tour

epitaph for aging

you are growing much too wise—
a sound like god said that to me—
grown wary tender for the pain
twilight kind about all hope
a humor for the once again
hard love softened into care
sunny numb for tragedy
dozing by a waiting lake
time a whisper in the wind

orphans

parents no they dare not die, how
dare they disappear into a
silence, forever gone a shield
of age against the world outside

left for living, young or old, if
a mother dies a baby whimpers,
a still face child with startled eyes,
strangers sitting on the edge of
chairs, sofas stiffened into
churchy pews

              a father tall sleeping
calm in a satin luxury,
working hands softly wooden resting
from all care, the worry of the world
faraway as breathing and a sigh

no longer son or daughter, if they are
dead, what shall we do now with warm
resentments, the sweet vexations,
the topsy-turvy heavy care
of parental children, the shame
of never having really loved
the ancient flesh which caused us and
the kitchen tedium that fed us years

lost

a penny or a love

some place in the world

but where oh where?

hiding in a rug

buried in a sigh

wanting to be found

wondering little boy

looking for a ball

man or woman staring

into an empty glass

a penny or a love

somewhere in this world

sparrow

a walking bird

with a perky head

hop touch the earth

bob for seeds

hidden somewhere

for the spring

flutter sudden

to a high limb

twitch a totter

with a quick tail

peck a feather

fly away forever

divorce

warm years cooling into stranger,

a sheath of wrinkled loneliness,

soiled wood skin, arms legs weak and

weary, a pain of cavern laughter

in wounded do-not-touch-me eyes

the brown edge of dying flowers,

dust sadly still on unread books,

last moment sigh of a setting sun

drizzle rain on an easter morning

timeless wait of a mirror pond

bewildered free on windy hill,

begging memory for a hug,

a surge of need for flesh somewhere,

a gloomy pride of mock survival

familiar faces

I know you, I'm sure I do,
we made love in a small canoe—
how do you do

I worked beside till you died
I heard about it and I sighed
I could have cried

I diapered you watched you grow,
anxious for what you need to know,
where are you though

mummy

now you listen all of you who were
once alive, a wounded antelope and
mozart with closed eyes, his quiet lips
humming violins in an unmarked grave,
anxious moths when morning came, bobby
burns in alcohol, hunted rabbits
in a bag and susans through the years
tinkling laughter behind tall bushes,
a tree that fell alone across a stream,
gurgling tease from here to god knows where

oh, please let me touch the tantalizing
neck of nefertiti, I want to hear
the call of ancient birds, pulsating
throbs of flesh warm ago, the voice
of jesus and sappho's sighs, I need
to talk with david hume and wonder hear
the thunder with trembling early man

we breathe our tender moment in
the sun and rain and love you once again
alive when in our fears we love ourselves

wooden days

ashamed that I am not alive
this very moment to the world
loving every shade of green
the still wait of space and clouds
nectar kiss of humming birds
high leaves in a playful breeze

worried eyes in a stranger face
helpless silence wanting love
the wild excitement of a child
lonely absence of the near ones
cool whispers from the quiet dead
and memories of an early joy

the niceties of thinking clear
bach in his organ sound alone
rembrandt in his golden gloom
fire wheel and right triangle
prayerful answer of an echo
and all the twinkle of the world

it's a pity

if I were god or nearly so
I would not let a pleasure end
nor find a place for any pain
if I were god or nearly so

if god were I or nearly so
he'd know the agony of care
the mother pain for someone's hurt
if god were I or nearly so

but he is what or where he is
and I am here or so it seems
and there's no way for him to know
how kind a god that I would be

terminal illness

a sweeter tedium than just living,
loving one's own flesh inward to
the bones, weary humor gazing
on the seeming well, a memory
of food and weather, forgotten
bouncey love on a slab of bed

lake dark tree by a stillness,
quietly breathing leaves in a
haze of sun, child wonder smile
at a fluttering bird and pool eyes
mirroring the light, echo voice
grateful for a touch of care

the awkward, apologetic talk
when leaving someone there and
coming lonely home to a presence

encyclopedia

they come back, the portrait dead,

intoned in organ words, mausoleum

cold preserved, with time softened

gratitude we bow to the slow creep

of knowing and the awe of art,

for us a primal and a costless gift,

while the wounded dead they lie

timeless in the dried blood

all there, the arrogance and

the trembling pride of trying,

maps of where we think we are,

the taunt of numbers and the webs

of wishing, solemn heavy books

too large for holding, without

a mask of smiles and laughter

from the edge of things

                          but oh

the mark of human kind in the glow

of genius, a mound of hope for vista

and the dancing sadness of all flesh

second wedding

a powder weather on their skin

uneasy hope in ritual promise

girl joy in a woman's face

boy grin on a heavy man

the beddy warmth of winter need

a lurk of lover's anger

and a calm of understanding

on smiling lips and fondling eyes

wise humor of an hour glass

sweet insistence of the muscle heart

a gratitude for accident

the blessing of a gentle breeze

devil girl

her eyes are nervous waiting
and her teeth a bite of love
wishing breasts and nipple hard
and her longing legs a twine

her voice cool and forest dark
speckles sun through teasing leaves
a sudden soft and tender body
when she thinks herself as winning

run wildly from the place you are
do not look and do not listen
but since living's worth the dying
tinkle echo to her laughter

second hand

ticky-tick the bleed of time
oozing my sweet life away
smile a whimsy at the hurry
too busy to look up at me

oh wait a little while
quietly like a meadow
with no wind in the trees
and a live bird painted still

nurse's eyes

I lay beside me in a bed
half awake for lurk of pain,
blanket fever mothering me,
staring heavy-eyed at time

she was standing oh so healthy
therapy in a dose of smile
stealing with a stick of glass
the hidden numbers of my warmth

as her fingers touched my pillow
I wandered love into blue eyes
and pouted wanting for her lips
but there was only science in
her gaze and white enamel care

balloon

I wish to be large balloon
held clinging to the earth
by anxious open faces

                  I want
to be a puff of air yearning
for the sky, a sway of bosomy
impatience to loft me clean
in space

              I would hover with a
tease over trees and human houses
moving with capricious winds
like the whims of early love

float on and on growing smaller
smile and sigh a vague farewell
old men would tell stories
of the balloon that got away

models

stilled in life

and boney lovely

expensively yours

and gracious whorey

unfreckled skin

perfumed a harem

silk a sigh

a tease of smile

eyes mirrored

into barren rooms

cosmetic lust

in coffin hope

sex

head full of wanting
tingle touch of flesh
grabby monkey frenzy
edgy wonder waiting

over shoulder loving
humming in the skin
smother human hair
night eyes in the dark

fading into lonely
soiled into stranger
tease of remembering
hollow gratitude

worn steps

shadow feet on waiting stone
softly human foot and shoe
caressing flesh and time away

joy or fear when stepping up
a meditation toeing down

the cold tears in the marble
and the hollow of a memory
deepen slowly like a grave

alas, poor yorick

socket eyes wiser still than hamlet
hollow contemplative humor
of time and hope and pulpy flesh,
the bite within the lippy smile
jaws teeth animal for panic food
cranial bone with a final thought

brood alone upon the world's incest
wound a girl for an early death
weave the words into sweet suicide—
oh, hamlet, there is laughter
in our grief, a twitch of life in
any pain, a comedy in dying

burned out

a widow loss of house and pans
the wounded smell of burnt wood
damp and sodden seep despair
charcoal funeral of ease
staring dead at memory things

a float of suicide laughing
wild, child in a fear of night,
dizzy whorl of a hollow cry
naked free in a fever womb
wooden ear for a grieving friend
and a whisper birth for once again

honorable men

faces honestly defacing
all semblances of doubt,
sly innocence deceiving
both itself and others,
knowledge boomeranging
death and ejaculating
hope, energy and matter—
triumph of the mind
and the certain end of man—
while the human voices
echo concrete into mobs

death masks for the living,
heart beats as muffled drums
processions of gold and
honors through hollow arching
halls, the puffy pride of
good ones, the villainy
of purity, time-bomb
on our thoughts and love

faded loveliness

she was, oh yes she was, a dresden
china girl, her skin enameled soft
and pink by god himself as artist,
small white teeth showed a smile of
shadow wrinkles gently human and
her laughter tinkled like a crystal
bell struck with a silver fork

when her years were gone, I saw her
in blue voile, sitting framed in
a high back wicker chair, a late
sun was coolly kind to the sky gray
of her hair, but the wounds were in
the underlining of her eyes and
in the dark trailing echo of her laugh

glimmer

veil of night shadowing
into day, stilled green
a painted world, a skein
of space and waking sky
softly loving sleepy eyes

pillow murmur of the dark
revery for a bedded girl
disheveled hair slippering
gray light into morning rooms
the whimper of a body love
jesting with the edge of time

just why

what can a blade of grass
know early on or buds
to be from wooden limbs,
the softening earth for
tender roots or spring
worms in the morning sun?

how do the metals lose
their winter cool to burn
surprise against the warm,
and why are we so late
to know the puppy love
of equinox and whim?

scarlet a

I envy all your agony,
embroidered sin on pointed
breasts, the twitching pain
of evil's good and thorny
love in nearby forests

for us a numby skin of
feel, a memory middle
in the fever, a faint
goodbye in every greeting,
with time an anesthesia,
bewilderment a friend

florist

speak petals in a scented flower
shop, mourn organ low for roses
funereal in glassy coffins,
child wonder at the shapes and
shades of green, god's eye for
color and the ah! design,
gardenias come from faraway
to soothe an anxious girl asleep,
lily women stately pouring
silver tea into small china
cups, carnations and the mums
warm skin waiting to be asked
to dance, a trace of men in
bark supported heavy leaves,
whimsy pots and selfish vases
mothering the loll of flowers

glimpses

all those flowers I will never see
and wing japans of butterflies,
galaxies beyond the human edge,
brook water in the thicket, girl
smiles and satin bodies linking
legs around the world in love,
art hands on primal stone and
metals asleep in silenced
earth, the boney hidden tease of
thought, reason twisting time and
space, the unheard noise of atom
talk, and the studied symbols of
mathematica dug slowly from the
catacombs of logic, the lurk of
rhythm and all the music of the
ear and mind, pain from long ago,
closed eyes and moaning mouths
deep alive in tomorrow's night

buttercup

wildflower girl
weed green eyes
skin white cream
mouth sweet teeth

vine cling arms
peony breasts
kneecap knees
earth sure feet

pouty high voice
mumble love
sudden bloom
winds away

capri

cloud high over deep blue water

balmily in love with a vague

forever, a breeze of tease for

ripple time and still white sails,

laughter from a stranger

sharing happy eyes and lips,

and from behind a silent tree

a child's noises of a game

you were a breath of flowers,

a glint of sun on open seas,

folding a loving body around

a rustle hum of thoughts,

an island of sweet tongue caprice

soft as warm skin in the night—

there was a hush about all parting

the sad swirl of lapping water

and the growing small of all capris

psychiatry

a surprise of cool over hot
summer skin, monster darkening
of blue-eyed skies, white blitz
of streak awareness against
the stranger creep of night,
grass and trees, paranoic still,
rushing from the wild hurry
of the wind, birds flying like
haunted leaves through the panic
air, touching padded droplets
soft panther paws for cunning
eyes, oh, suddenly the suicide
of falling water, laughter from
the ancient seas flowing in the
body's love, then the wandering
sadness of departing rain,
lonely in the wet of time,
a new world dustless bright and
vivid sane, a tender vision
painted on the green, sweet post
coital weariness and a sigh
echoing through the emptiness

by the water's edge

shadow lashes on still eyes—

long ago a prance of girl,

white teeth biting into love,

bird wings in her smile of sighs

glisten on her summer skin

yield of warm breast to my hand

wet leaves drifting slowly by,

water-light in ripple gleam,

inner hum of memories

sweet weariness and a twinge,

squared boldly for the world again

shadow lashes on still eyes

resurrection

I died, now that was quite a while ago,
a bleed of treason and a breathless
heart and I was done for, paid a fare
across a night black river the greeks
and romans knew and ghostly wandered
through remembered bruising hurt and
soft evasive love in frigid time

winter still in spring a hyacinth
was purple smiling in the early cool
and tulips offered cups for blessing
wine, a running child fell and cried
for mother touch and ran again into
the world, a scurry of a flock of birds
excited sunlight in the sleeping air,
now I am edge alive for care or wound

dead enemy

his death was never once my wish
I did not needle pain into
his waxen image, his tick in
time did not shorten mine

what, not when he was, I loathed,
his brutish view of human kind
the slime and ooze of his deceit
cold hands around a breathing throat

now casket pale in innocence
his death in everyone a plea
for closing of all open eyes
owed to the dead for living

mentally retarded

bewildered parent lovers staring
at a baby, warm innocence
with water eyes deceived into
broken life by demonic genes,
chancy molecules in double
helixes of brutal humor,
the flower sentiments of hope
plucked from a tender pride and
powdery joy

     years upon, a mother
woman and a courage man, care and
love beyond the sting of vanity,
the shy malaise of those who look,
a calm of sea a wait of sky
and the hurt too deep for pain

hysteria

it was a day to lose your mind
cold clouds and a flash of sun
wind swirling thoughts around
gossip leaves whispering rumors

nervous shadows under bushes
laughter trembling in the sky
echoes from a cavern longing
grey tears for a gasping need

weary wildness in the arms
hot love for a stranger waiting
anxious nowhere far and near
weepy for a cuddling mother

bars closed

he wandered shadowy on walls,

lulled a moon into a desert

love, pity crying two a. m.

for a sleepy town, silent screams

in nightmare bodies, sick whores

with breasted money, lean dogs

clanking cans, dead people shoring

strength for ghostly work, new life

babies morning hungry, cold traffic

lights blinking law, watcher bulbs

in dim lit shops, parking spaces

beggar waiting, steely bank vaults

teasing greed, drug stores smiling

anesthesia, the nauseous warmth of

always dying, clown humor of sidewalks

dancing, numb alone in whirled despair,

absorbed by the dark side of a tree

pianist

tendril fingers caressing sound

like sunlight leaves from hidden winds,

bone chords from the inner thunder

rumbling through the darkened air,

arpeggios the leaping deer, scurry

runs of shadow mice, muscle joy

of body music rushing waterfall

into the world, pianissimo

a lover's lips on womanly hair,

schizoid hands folded in prayer

fragile

downy low her whisper voice
petunia petal of a girl
trembling for a butterfly

filigree her arms and legs
willowy her golden hair
dusky eyes from faraway

tinkle laughter into pain,
her love a viola grieving,
softly open for a hurt

dust

a wisp of powder on

the stillness of things,

old lace for grey voices,

cushions softly dying,

mourning black on silver

candlesticks, piano keys

browning quietly out of

tune, shawl of linen sun

warming corners of a room,

child eyes of bric-a-brac,

lonely waiting rocking chairs

spring caprice

the who and owl
of the windy howl

the swish of trees
and the fear of leaves

a scowl of cloud
earth freshly plowed

the rush of rain
for breath again

middens

so you found my jawbone
and my woman's pots,
your eyes widened
by thick lenses
brushing time carefully
away, a cry of wonder
for our art in things,
the miracles of our
heavy stones blunting
your metallic blades,
the honest grotesque of
our gods mocking yours

when your flesh is bone
and love a fissure
in the sand, pride a
stillness and time
a silence in the
earth, eyeless we will
gaze and listen to
the digging and the
whisper of the brushes

spring leaves

just teen girls

with button breasts

boy man with a

foolish smile

violin fingers

on the e string

tremolo with

early joy

bird song on

a tender twig

cool warm air

for a wing

wrong number

a voice, a child's

close and far as

echo— oh, no,

wrong number,

goodbye now

little stranger

fare thee well

no one whom you

meant to call

could love you so

plants

how still and buddha calm you are,

a veil of smile on moving things,

stems contemplative green

quieting the breath of color

the shy unfolding of your leaves,

stillness of our human time

hidden from an anxious eye,

wisdom in a subtle hush

little monks of death in life,

sandal feet on sacred earth,

silence in delusive flowers

a garden scent of prayers

winter forest

the woods are winter bare, come,
walk with me through soldier trees
and crunchy leaves mothering the
orphan earth, whimsy hold the hatted
acorns, oak-hard sure of spring,
finger grip the slatted cones,
cabins for pioneering pines,
breathe the cold air icy round
the stiffly waiting lippy buds,
look, a squirrel, puffed in fur,
busy with a winter chore, a bird
on a barren limb, like a memory
in frost, and the sun's chilly
glare on frozen cheeks, courage
bones laughing at summer flesh

rain clouds

damp shroud in a dirge of sky

cold grey of a widow grieving

child smile in a glint of sun

timid sway of barren limbs

sheen of chill on grass and stones

wet horses in a swampy meadow

hollow loneliness in time

mother warm in window houses

dna

twist a life, o double helix,

spiral agony or twirly

gifts, whispering genes

coding destiny as grecian

masks, jumpy ions into

crippled bones or taunts

of loveliness, a frenzy

tarantella of chance,

a microscopic mockery

of hope, cathedral

spires for a dicey god

druthers

going this way once more around
these are my offers— to be
a mathematician, symbol keen,
lonely at the edge of reason,
or a musician black illiterate
dripping music from his fingertips

nothing middling, I won't be teased
half alive by zero sums and
numbers larger than my eyes,
mute sounds on waiting strings,
echo melodies too often sung,
pulses deaf beneath the skin

reason knife or bleed of sound
or I'll not wager flesh again

rejected lover

he crowded her back into the

nonexistence where she was

before they met, ghostly far

the veil of her face, the soft

haunt of her breasts and legs,

the soprano laughing echo

of her voice through the lake

and woods of dreamy care

sky and world and hollow air,

stranger thoughts greeting bows

with lonesome smiles, deaf-mute

friends, squirrels clinging to

a tree, humor with alerted stares,

walking nowhere, loose and weary,

his salad memories tart and forky,

and nursing time coldly cheerful

rosebud in bloom

purple-hair old ladies
wooden boney memories
spritely prim on spring
warm days, a fear of chill
in every breeze, voices
softly hoarse and laughter
echoing through empty
houses, sudden girl in jewel
eyes peeping under flower
curls, crinkled lips waiting
a remembered lover or
a grandchild's perching visit
feathering a birdie kiss

park bench

I have fallen in love
with the end of it all,
watching the whimsy spray
on a fountain pool, bird
wing hurry in summery
air, the ripple humor
of a languid lake, infant
leaves in early spring,
first-time children laughing
young and the doggy sleep
near an owning voice

the painted stillness of
waiting people, staring blind
at the world around, sunlight
on the lawn of memories,
twiggy fingered puppy
lovers swaying music in
a happy float of fever,
the quiet glee of being
alive, with a mourn of time,
the shy gift of wanting,
a smile of soft forgiving

easel

early morning and

in evening light

a painter's world,

the green of green

and houses white

in stilled vision,

skies the glow of

costume color,

puffy breasts and

feathery art

moment waiting

picture birds,

wistful eyes and

palette envy,

forgiving god

were I

were I the poet of our time,

pounding echo to its beat,

bloody cheered by violence,

sibling to the psycho sex,

love but the flesh while it

is warm, gadget bored by

reason's gifts, teasing death

the laughter of plutonium

and the giggle of our speed,

I would disappear into the

silence underneath the noise,

where pain and love are children,

the spring earth soft and near again,

and all we are a darkened fear

barefoot

naked feet on remembered
grass, mini jungles gibbering
monkey chatter, morning earth
awaking toes, wet or warm,
lover sand for lazing love,
mumu bodies sheathing yawns
of flesh desire, pulpy tender
heels touching boney ground,
brook pebbles inventing primal
dances, primordial ooze and
cloy of mud, death masks of
footprints, stilled in time

anyone

they come from the thicket
of nowhere and leave for a
restless gleam, with a hurt
so deep it ends in laughter

there's an infancy in
opening eyes, a toy
in a sparkle or shine,
tease in a tinkle of love

however it was, a wound
cutting the warm child flesh
aged a new life into old,
squinting after once ago

bird envy

warbling bird in a tree
throaty happy wing and air,
moment perch and feathers
fluffy in a sway of leaves

whimsy flying to a limb,
twitch head for a listen,
balance in a quick tail,
touchy ballet on the ground

me a wing of wishing
on a twig of somewhere,
a warble in my wanting,
a flutter to a tree

death bed

dying he knew the absurdity
of having lived, the faded
whimsy of a child at play,
the squirm of school and
early love in a muffled
body, fingers on the crisp
of money, stolen power from
a motor, faint recall of
honeymoon with a woman now
a sister, the flash of children
born and gone and the tedium
of days until the echo from
the cavern of a wisdom sighed
a laughter in a grimace
and the wait breathed slowly

rose petals

a girl a flower in her hand
and spring a whispering bud,
laughter in her opening mouth,
bird chatter on a leafing twig

sky light halo round her hair,
day stars remembering night,
the burn of sun on loving skin
and the tingle tangle of desire

senile fantasy

he was waiting in an airport
for a terminal flight
                        when
a smile of incidental
love flickered in a young girl's
face

    a rush of still believing
smoothed the wisdom in his eyes

found a gulf stream warm against
an island chill
                        until a mock
of laughter from an ancient boy
wreathed a sweetened sad regret
round the awareness of his hope

sky song

ballet tutu

rain drops

on a pond

glisten

pearl eyes

in the grass

bird hop

a wet twig

swaying

sun smile

peep around

a cool cloud

fear and flight

like a frightened bird you fly
a hundred times your size away,
flapping frantic wings to clutch
safe afar a swaying branch

your twitching head and beaded
eyes do not remember me a noise,
no glance of memory warm
to soothe the edge of care

other birds with feathers yours
wing their way in air half mine,
chirping stranger love at me,
but you for me forever gone

autumn's coming

arthritic bones and birds
all know when autumn's near,
leaves and grass and summer
flowers, window panes and
concrete bridges, people
eyes with chilly smiles,
the sky with frosty clouds,
fingers on cold metal,
feet on hardened ground,
lovers cuddling for the
winter, reddened leaves
on grieving trees and night
a stranger in the dark

cancer

frightened by the silence of the flesh,
ashamed of living on, I watched you die,
whispering your name into the catacomb
sedation, touching the warmth of you
while still it lasted, remembering
your smiles of whim and joy, your eyes
upon the world, the music of your voice

the hush of death a veil of smile at
book and brain, the stillness of the
hour hand a memory, grief a lonely walk
around a winter lake, yet you were never
more alive than now— an agony of care
and muted speech, I am part of all your
dying, waiting bravely for my time

once

once long ago or now or never
time grew tired of happening,
the face of clocks were sleepy
and the sand in hour glasses
burned with fever and mirage

birds were stilled in flight
and echoes waited in the air
sun and moon were one at last
flowers were always in bloom
and children ah! forever young

final parting

girl on a high ledge

fingering goodbye and

me in a small boat

drifting to sea

                              the cool

breath of a warm wind

embalming farewell

sunlight lover caressing

her hair

                a shawl of soft

cloud

                and her grey eyes

the horizon faraway

peering

ah, yes, the skeleton inside a hope,

x-ray bones beneath soft flesh

bacteria fermenting in the dark

the lurk of ailment in the genes,

sudden near in stranger eyes

quirks of seeming most alive,

skin in love with early spring

summer woman of the flowers

evening star before it's night

children's faces in their sleep

flakes

star designs in
falling silence
puffing white
the frozen brown

whisper fingers
on ice faces
soft cold scoops
in stony hands

trees and bushes
blooming snow
children grass
tucked in winter

distance

they stand at far ends of bridges

waving arms of valley love,

voices swept by winds into

grimaced silence, tear-laugh eyes

weeping nearness faraway,

the tease of panic need,

open lips a mock of words,

flesh apart a bleed of time

on wait and hope, oh, scream

an echo, hug a sky, make

loneliness a fierce embrace

icy chirp

flurry snow

on april green,

peeking leaves

in winter air,

brooding sky

cheeky cold,

season birds

chilled in frost,

whimsy snow

teasing grass

whitecaps

beach sand girl bodies
lolling in a lover
sun, fever cool boys
jockey ready strong

shore lapping sea dreams
wetting up to grass,
seaweed hair stringy
on the sleepy sand

seashell murmurs
memories of waves,
warm skin laughter
under echo sky

dogwood

spring flowers
on winter trees
pink and white
ja-pan-ese

hair-do bloom
frill on bark
may day love
dancing park

tissue quaint
fragile sweet
slanted eyes
birdie tweet

excellency

no aristocratic sway
like the breast of birds
no mace of power
like the clutch of twigs

stand rigid for a holbein,
gleam empire in a stare,
a robin with a worm's
more royal in his pride

let alexander dream
of parcel land and sea,
birds with a flip of wing
possess a world of air

requiem

grief for all the dying—
discolored petals of a rose
wrinkles for an ivory neck
aging dogs in willow shade

poet's death of echo words
mozart buried in the rain
rembrandt stilled in gold
la commedia è finita

ivy ruins of ancient gods
night light from a star
martinis for a faded love
corpse eyes for a face

if then

were time the anesthesia for
the hurt, dead men would be
live ones, winged birds still
in flight, fallen leaves on
greening trees, rigor mortis
love a wiggle of desire

if being numb were living
and wooden things were cotton,
stillness a capricious wind,
muted wait a babbling child,
then night would be morning
and death another breath

epitaph for a nobody

he longed to leave a scratch
on the hard surface of
the world, hear his name an
echo in the caverns
of dead waiting, girl
bodies wiggling gratitude,
the clap of hands in noisy
prayer, twinkle stars for
approving gods, sleepy
pride forever certain

instead the pulpy dying
of his flesh, the humor
of humility and the sighs
of vague remembering,
purr and rumble of a
rented hearse, the anon
of a skeleton, eye socket
hollow time, boney friends
with talents gone, cold
love in wedded shrouds

dry grass

in a garden and let me say
we are in the cool of autumn,
the iris are droopy brown
remembering their lacey days,
peonies are sallow women
grieving for their fallen bosoms,
marigolds— I do declare!—
think they're still in summer bloom,
would you look at those geraniums
redhead young on chilly nights,
petunias now are sweet old ladies
winking at the grocery boy,
me, I'm a weed awaiting winter,
crisp and dry and cackling on,
but I'm a flower in the fall,
with none of spring to grieve for

sudden death of a child

all at once the living sounds
are silence in the womb,
sunlight through a breeze
of curtain sadly whispers
early voices, a child's
laughter echoes through
the grief, toys are epitaphs
of love, clothing breathing
warm, until parental dying
in the hollow of a heart
binds the living and the dead
in a twilight of remembrance

bye

look, mums, flowers

baby legs

yes

blue flowers

blue flowers

god is a nice man isn't he mums

small shoes

baby legs

blue flowers

alphabetical list of titles

alphabetical list of titles